LIFE'S LITTLE PEACHES, PEARS, PLUMS & PRUNES COOKBOOK:

101 Fruit Recipes

by Joan Bestwick

Life's Little Peaches, Pears,
Plums & Prunes Cookbook
101 Fruit Recipes

by Joan Bestwick

Copyright 2001
by Avery Color Studios, Inc.
ISBN# 1-892384-11-6
Library of Congress Card #

Published by
Avery Color Studios, Inc.
Gwinn, Michigan 49841

Cover photo by Michael Prokopowicz,
Michael's Photographics, Gwinn, Michigan

Proudly printed in U.S.A.

Table of Contents

I would like to dedicate this book to God and all of the blessings that he has given to our family. To Judy Kerr from Friske's Orchards in Atwood, Michigan for suggesting this book to Avery Color Studios, Inc. as my 4th book. God bless you Judy, you're a beautiful woman. To my mentor and side kick Rosalee Kakish, a great woman of God and teacher. Also to my oldest best friend in the world of almost 30 years, Faith Ann Schultz and to Crystal Hope, Arrow Harmony and Jason Paul.

ello,

In my childhood we had a small orchard on the farm, but I remember most fondly the old pear tree that stood in front of my Grandpa Manning's meat market, and it is still standing there today. We would climb that tree and spy on the customers. The pears also made great live grenade bombs which would sometimes get us in trouble, then we would have to pick rocks in the fields. I also remember in the spring watching the bees have field days in the fruit trees. It was always fun eating the fresh fruit, the juice would run down your chin, which was a good excuse to go swimming in the ponds.

I feel very privileged when I look around today at the high tech world and compare it to my childhood memories, where we had to depend on the land for food to carry us through the year. I was very blessed to have lived this life and that my parents taught me how to be very creative in the kitchen so we would not be bored with our food. I always thought we were poor but when I look at life now, we were very rich in love, memory and God. Thank you Mom and Dad for teaching me the real meaning of life so that my family is blessed today.

Joan

Peaches: There are basically two types of peaches. The freestones and clingstones. The freestone types; the flesh separates easily from the pit. The cling-stone type clings tightly to the pit. The freestone types are preferred for eating and freezing. The cling-stone types are used basically for canning. Clingstones keep longer than freestones. Peaches have 40 calories for a medium peach, 10 mg of Vitamin C and 190 mg of potassium. A good source of fiber. Typically 1 pound is about 3-4 medium peaches; 1 lb = 2-1/2 cups sliced, 2-1/4 cups chopped, or 1-1/2 cups pureed. To buy peaches, choose them with a yellowish to golden color. They should be firm or slightly "give" with a little pressure. To ripen them fast, place them in a paper bag, close and keep at room temperature, check daily. Before eating, wash fruit to remove the "fuzz." Store in refrigerator 3 to 5 days. When eating peaches fresh, serve at room temperature for best flavor. If a recipe calls for a peeled peach the best way to peel it is to dip the peach in boiling water for about 20 -30 seconds. Remove with a slotted spoon, dip in cold water. The skin will peel more easily.

Pears: A medium pear is 100 calories and has 4 grams of fiber. They are high in potassium, 210 mg and contain 7 mg of Vitamin C. A pear is ripe when you apply a little pressure with your thumb near the base of the stem and it yields slightly. If it's not ripe yet, place your pear in a brown paper bag and let stand at room temperature.

Some of the most favorite pears are the Bartlett and D'Anjou. 1 pound is about 3 medium pears; 1 lb = 3 cups sliced.

Plums: Plums have 40 calories in a medium size, 110 mg of potassium, 10 mg of Vitamin C. Plums are a fruit that can be used for eating fresh, canning, freezing, jams and jellies. To tell if a plum is ripe apply a gentle pressure to the fruit with your thumb and it should feel soft. If you're not going to eat your fresh ripe fruit right away store it in your refrigerator.

Prunes: Prunes are a dried plum and may help reduce your risk of heart disease and certain cancers. Prunes should be soaked in water until swollen. Prunes have 100 calories per 1-1/2 ounce serving (about 5 dried plums) and are naturally low in sodium, fat and are cholesterol free. They include essential nutrients such as beta carotene, dietary fiber and potassium.

To prevent fruit from browning after slicing and before serving, dip the fruit pieces in a little lemon juice or orange juice.

PEACHES

*Cooking is like advice, you should
try it before you feed it to others.*

Baked Peaches with Raspberry Sauce

1/2 of a 10-ounce package frozen raspberries in syrup
1-1/2 teaspoons lemon juice
2 medium fresh peaches, peeled, pitted and halved
5 teaspoons brown sugar
1/4 teaspoon ground cinnamon
1/4 teaspoon sugar
3/4 tablespoon butter or margarine

In a blender or food processor mix raspberries and lemon juice until pureed. Strain and discard the seeds. Cover and chill. Preheat oven to 350°. In a baking dish place the peaches pitted center side up. In a bowl, combine the sugars and cinnamon. Place this mixture in each peach center and then place a 1/4 teaspoon of butter in each peach center. Cover the baking dish with foil and bake for 20-30 minutes. The peach will be heated through and the center melted. To serve, spoon the raspberry sauce over each peach in a serving dish.

Peach Salsa

1/2 cup peach preserves
1/2 - 3/4 cup chopped peaches peeled and pitted
1/4 cup sliced green onions
2 tablespoons finely chopped jalapeno peppers
1 tablespoon fresh lemon juice
1 or 2 cloves of garlic, crushed
1/4 teaspoon grated fresh ginger (optional)
Dash of salt and pepper

Combine all of the ingredients in a bow and mix well. This can be served warm or cold. It is good warm over beef or pork.

Peach Bread

1 cup fresh peach puree
3/4 cup sugar
1/4 cup butter or margarine
1-3/4 cups flour
1/2 teaspoon cinnamon
1/2 teaspoon baking powder
1/2 teaspoon baking soda
1/8 teaspoon salt
1 egg
1/2 teaspoon vanilla
1/4 cup chopped walnuts or pecans

Preheat oven to 325°. In a bowl, cream the sugar and butter. In a different bowl, mix together all of the dry ingredients, then add the butter mixture, peach puree, egg and vanilla. Mix well. Add the nuts and mix. Pour the batter into a greased loaf pan and bake 55-60 minutes until done. Remove from pan and cool on rack. Try some peach butter on the warm peach bread, Yum!

Peach Leather

This is an old recipe from way back.

1 pound of peaches
1/4 pound of sugar

Take your peaches and peel, pit and chop. Place the peaches in a heavy pot and start cooking them down. A little water can be added at the start. Add sugar. As the peaches cook, they will soften, mash them as they cook. Cook over low heat until it is like a thick smooth paste. Keep stirring and cook for a good hour. When done spread the mixture on a greased cookie sheet to cool. Grandma set this in the sun to dry. When dry, roll it up in wax paper or foil to store. Place in a glass jar and store in a cool dry cupboard. It will keep for a long time.

Peach Raspberry Jam

2-2/3 cups peaches, pitted, peeled and finely chopped
1-1/2 cups raspberries
3 cups sugar
1-1/2 teaspoons lemon juice

Over low heat in a large heavy kettle, combine all of the ingredients. Cook, stirring occasionally until the sugar is dissolved and the mixture bubbles. Bring this to a full rolling boil for about 15 minutes, stirring constantly. Remove this from the heat, skim off the foam. Pour this mixture into hot sterile jars and seal. Process in a hot water bath for 15 minutes. Makes 5 half pints.

Peaches and Cream

4 cups fresh peaches, pitted and sliced
1 package (8 ounces) cream cheese softened
1/4 cup confectioners sugar
2 -3 tablespoons light cream
1/2 teaspoon vanilla extract
1/4 teaspoon almond extract

Place your peaches in serving bowls. Using a mixer or food processor, mix the cream cheese and confectioners sugar. Then add the cream and extract and process until smooth. Pour this mixture over your fruit.

Sweet Peach Pilaf

3/4 to 1 cup sliced peaches peeled, pitted (fresh or canned)
2-1/4 cups cooked white rice prepared (keep hot)
3 tablespoons butter
1/2 teaspoon cinnamon
1/4 cup brown sugar
1/8 teaspoon salt
1 cup cream whipped or 2 cups prepared whipped topping
1/2 cup walnuts, chopped
Walnut halves and maraschino cherries for garnish

In a pan prepare enough rice to make 2-1/4 cups. When you add the rice to the boiling water also add the peaches. Cover and let stand for 15 minutes. After it has set for 15 minutes add the butter, cinnamon, brown sugar and salt. Mix well. Let this mixture cool. When this mixture is cool add the cream that has been whipped until fluffy. Fold this in or use 2 cups prepared whipped topping. Then top with nuts. Garnish the rice mixture with walnut halves and maraschino cherries.

Chicken with Peach and Pineapple Sauce

3 pounds of chicken, cut up
1-8 ounce can crushed pineapple undrained
1 cup orange juice
1/2 cup raisins
1/2 cup sliced almonds
1/4 teaspoon ground cinnamon
1/4 teaspoon ground cloves (optional)
2 cups canned peaches, pureed
Salt and pepper

In a large fry pan place the chicken, pineapple, orange juice, raisins, almonds, cinnamon and cloves. Bring to a boil, then simmer partly covered for 45 minutes, turning the chicken occasionally. Add the peach puree to the pan and stir until well blended. Simmer partially covered for an additional 15 minutes or until the chicken is tender and the sauce is slightly thickened. Season with salt and pepper. Serves 4. This dish is very good with couscous because of its nutty flavor.

Peach Upside-Down Cake

1/2 cup butter or margarine, melted
1/2 cup packed brown sugar
10-12 peach halves, fresh or canned, peeled and pitted
10-12 maraschino cherries, halved (optional)
1 cup coconut
1/4 cup chopped pecans (optional)
2 eggs
2/3 cup sugar
1/2 teaspoon almond extract
1/4 cup peach juice or water
1 cup all purpose flour
1 teaspoon baking powder
1/4 teaspoon salt

Preheat oven to 350°. In a 9-inch baking pan pour the butter and sprinkle the brown sugar. Arrange the peach halves cut side down. Place the cherries around the peaches; sprinkle the coconut and nuts around the peaches also. Set aside. In a mixing bowl, beat the eggs until thick and lemon colored. Then gradually beat in the sugar. Add the extract and juice or water. In a separate bowl combine the flour, baking powder and salt. Add this to the egg mixture and mix well. Carefully pour this mixture over the peaches. Bake for 50-60 minutes or until done. Cool 10 minutes and invert the cake onto a serving plate. 6-8 servings.

Cottage Cheese Peach Pie

Crust:

1 cup walnuts, chopped
1/2 cup butter or margarine, softened
3/4 cup all purpose flour
1/2 cup packed brown sugar
1/2 teaspoon vanilla extract

Filling:

4 cups peaches, pitted, peeled and chopped
1 cup plain yogurt
1 cup small-curd cottage cheese
1/2 cup crushed pineapple, drained
1/4 cup shredded coconut

Preheat oven to 350°. In a medium bowl, combine the nuts, butter, flour, brown sugar and vanilla with a fork. In a 9-inch pie plate press this mixture to form a crust. Bake for 10-15 minutes until brown. Cool on a wire rack. After cooled, place the peaches into the pie shell. In a blender or food processor mix the yogurt and cottage cheese until smooth. Add the pineapple and blend. Pour this mixture over the fruit. Sprinkle with coconut. Chill for a few hours before serving. If desired decorate the pie with fruit. Serves 12.

Peach Blueberry Cobbler

2 cups fresh peaches
1/2 cup sugar
4 teaspoons quick cooking tapioca
2 teaspoons fresh lemon juice
1 cup fresh blueberries
dash of nutmeg

Cobbler:
1 cup all purpose flour
2 tablespoons sugar
1-1/2 teaspoons baking powder
1/8 teaspoon salt
1 teaspoon grated lemon rind
1/4 cup butter or margarine
1/2 cup evaporated milk

Combine the peaches, sugar, tapioca, lemon juice and blueberries in a pan over medium heat. Bring this mixture to a boil and cook for a couple of minutes until thickened. Add the nutmeg and stir, remove from the heat and place in a 1-1/2 quart baking dish. In a bowl combine the flour, sugar, baking powder, salt and lemon rind. Then add the butter. Using a fork or pastry blender, blend until the mixture resembles corn meal. Add the milk and stir until the dough is moistened and mixed. Drop by tablespoons over the hot filling. Bake at 400° for 25-30 minutes or until the top is golden brown. Serves 8.

Oriental Chicken and Peaches

3 pounds of chicken, cut up
Salt and pepper
1 large onion, sliced
1 cup ketchup
1 tablespoon honey
2 tablespoons soy sauce
1 cup water
1 large green bell pepper cut up into 1 inch pieces
2 peaches, peeled and sliced into eighths

Preheat oven to 450°. Sprinkle the chicken with salt and pepper. Place the skin side up in a lightly greased 2-1/2 quart baking dish. Bake for 20 minutes. Remove the chicken from the oven and place onion slices on top of the meat. In a small bowl, blend the ketchup, honey, soy sauce and water. Pour this mixture over the chicken. Cover and bake for 30 minutes. Remove from oven and add the green pepper and peaches over the chicken. Spoon the sauce over the chicken, peppers and peaches. Cover and bake an additional 15 minutes.

Peach Turnovers

2 cups all purpose flour
2 tablespoons sugar
1/2 teaspoon salt
1 stick unsalted butter
3 tablespoons solid
   vegetable shortening

2 eggs
3 ripe peaches
1 tablespoon vanilla or
   almond extract
2 tablespoons seedless
   red raspberry jam

In a large bowl, combine the flour, sugar and salt. Cut in the butter and shortening until the mixture resembles coarse meal. Beat one of the eggs and add it to the flour mixture. Gather the dough into a ball. If some of the flour does not adhere, sprinkle in a few drops of cold water. Divide the dough in half and flatten into two 6-inch disks. Wrap well and refrigerate for at least 30 minutes or even a day ahead of time. When ready to use let the dough stand at room temperature until a little softened. Peel the peaches, pit and dice the peaches in small pieces. Place in a bowl and add the extract, toss and coat. Let the peaches macerate tossing occasionally for 30 minutes. To assemble the turnovers, preheat the oven to 400°. On a lightly floured surface, roll out one of the pastry discs to 1/4 inch thick. With a circular pastry cutter, cut out 3 circles 5 inches in diameter. Leaving a 1/2 inch border all around, paint each circle with 1/2 teaspoon raspberry jam. Then over the jam add 1/6 of the peaches. Moisten the unpainted rims with water, fold over and press the edges of the pastry together. Crimp with a fork to seal. Repeat with the remaining pastry, jam and peaches to make 3 more turnovers. Arrange the turnovers on a heavy cookie sheet. Beat the remaining egg with 1/2 tablespoon water and brush this over the pastry. Bake the turnovers in the middle of the oven for about 20 minutes or until the pastry is a light golden brown. Transfer to a rack and let cool.

Peach Soup

2 cups peaches, peeled and pitted
2 tablespoons lemon juice
2 tablespoons sugar
2 cups white grape juice
1 small cinnamon stick
1/8 teaspoon almond extract

In a blender or food processor puree the peaches. In a bowl pour in the peaches and mix in the lemon juice and sugar and let set. In a saucepan, heat the white grape juice and cinnamon stick to a boil and then simmer 2 minutes. Strain and mix in the extract. Mix this into the peaches and chill. Serve chilled.

Peach Sauce

2 tablespoons butter
3 tablespoons sugar
1 tablespoon lemon juice
3 peaches peeled, pitted and sliced
1 teaspoon vanilla

In a saucepan, heat the butter, sugar and lemon juice until it boils. Add the peaches to this and cook 5 minutes stirring often. Remove this mixture from the heat and stir in the vanilla. This is great over ice cream and cakes.

Peach Crumb

1/2 cup flour
1/2 cup rolled oats
1/2 cup brown sugar
1/4 teaspoon nutmeg
1/4 teaspoon salt
1/2 teaspoon cinnamon
1/4 cup butter or margarine
4 cups of peaches peeled, pitted and sliced thin
2 tablespoons water
1 teaspoon lemon juice

Preheat oven to 350°. In a bowl, mix the first six ingredients well. Then cut in the butter with a fork until the mixture crumbles. In another bowl, toss the peaches, water and lemon juice. Place the peaches in a greased 8-inch baking dish, then top with the crumb mixture and pat it down. Bake for 45 minutes until golden brown and bubbly.

Spiced Peaches

2 quarts small peaches
Whole cloves
2-1/2 cups brown sugar
1 cup cider vinegar
1 cinnamon stick, broken

In a stock pot boil water. Place peaches in the boiling water and scald them. Drain and peel. Stick a clove in each peach. In your stock pot add the sugar, vinegar, cinnamon and bring to a boil. Then add the peaches and cook until tender, about 10 minutes. In hot sterile jars pack the peaches and syrup. Seal and hot water bath for 5 minutes. Makes 5 pints.

Pecan Peach Pie

1/4 cup butter
1/4 cup brown sugar
3 tablespoons flour
2 teaspoons lemon juice
4 cups sliced peaches
3/4 cup pecans
1 9-inch unbaked prepared pie shell

In a saucepan over medium heat cook butter, sugar and flour until thickened, using a whisk. Add the lemon juice. Fold in the peaches to this mixture and coat. Pour the peaches into the pie shell. Sprinkle the top of the peaches with the pecans. Bake at 250° for 40-45 minutes.

Frozen Peach Melba Pie

1 pound fresh peaches, pitted, peeled and sliced
3/4 cup light corn syrup
1 tablespoon lemon juice
1 pint raspberry sherbet, softened
1 cup vanilla ice cream, softened
1 9-inch graham cracker crust

In a food processor, place the peaches, corn syrup, lemon juice and puree. Fold 1 cup of the peach puree into the raspberry sherbet. Pour this mixture into the graham cracker crust. Freeze 1 hour or until firm. Fold the remaining 1 cup of peach puree into the vanilla ice cream. Pour this over the raspberry layer. Cover and freeze until firm. If desired, garnish with pecan slices.

Peach and Cherry Sauce

4 large peaches, sliced and pitted
1/2 cup maraschino cherry sauce
1/2 cup green grapes, cut in half if desired

Maraschino Cherry Sauce:
3/4 cup sugar
1 tablespoon cornstarch
1/4 cup light corn syrup
1/4 cup maraschino cherry juice
1/4 cup strained orange juice
1/2 cup of water

For the maraschino cherry sauce: in a heavy saucepan, combine 3/4 cup sugar and 1 tablespoon cornstarch. Stir in 1/4 cup light corn syrup, 1/4 cup maraschino cherry juice, 1/4 cup strained orange juice and 1/2 cup of water. Bring this to a boil and cook 3 minutes until the sauce is clear and slightly syrupy. Remove from the heat. Add some chopped maraschino cherries. Refrigerate. To finish the recipe, combine the peaches, 1/2 cup of the cherry sauce and grapes if desired. Store in refrigerator until serving. Serves 4.

Peach Honey

1 large orange de-seeded
12 large peaches, peeled and pitted
Sugar

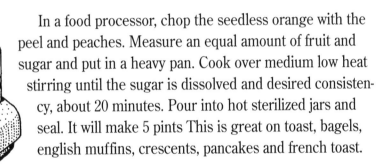

In a food processor, chop the seedless orange with the peel and peaches. Measure an equal amount of fruit and sugar and put in a heavy pan. Cook over medium low heat stirring until the sugar is dissolved and desired consistency, about 20 minutes. Pour into hot sterilized jars and seal. It will make 5 pints This is great on toast, bagels, english muffins, crescents, pancakes and french toast.

Peach Dumplings

3 cups sifted flour
4 teaspoons baking powder
1 teaspoon salt
2/3 cup shortening
1 cup milk
6 large ripe peaches, peeled
12 tablespoons sugar
1/4 teaspoon ground nutmeg
6 teaspoons honey
6 teaspoons butter
2 tablespoons sugar

Preheat oven to 400°. In a bowl sift together the flour, baking powder and salt. Cut in the shortening with a fork until the mixture is crumbly. Stir in the milk and make dough. Knead the dough slightly on a lightly floured surface. Divide the dough into sixths. Roll each piece of dough 1/8 inch thick and cut into a 7 inch square and place a peach in the center of each square. Top each peach with 2 tablespoons of sugar, a dash of nutmeg and 1 teaspoon honey. Moisten the edges of the dough with water and fold up each peach firmly pressing edges to seal. Place the dumplings in a 13 x 9 x 2 inch baking pan. Dot each with 1 teaspoon butter; sprinkle evenly with 2 tablespoons sugar. Bake about 35-40 minutes until golden brown. Serves 6.

Peach Apricot Cobbler

1/2 cups granulated sugar
2 tablespoons cornstarch
1 (1pound 13 ounce) can sliced peaches, drained and reserve juice
1 (10-1/2 ounce) can apricot halves, drained and reserve juice
1 tablespoon butter
1/2 teaspoon ground cinnamon
1/4 teaspoon ground nutmeg

Topping:
1/2 cup all purpose flour
1/2 cup granulated sugar
1/4 teaspoon baking powder
1/4 teaspoon salt
2 tablespoons butter, softened
1 large egg

Preheat oven to 400°. In a medium saucepan, mix together the sugar and cornstarch. Over medium heat stir in 1/2 cup each of the reserved peach and apricot juice. Pour slowly and whisk until the mixture boils and thickens, about 2 minutes. Remove from the heat. Stir in the butter, cinnamon and nutmeg. Add the fruit. Spoon the fruit mixture into a 1-1/2 quart casserole dish.

To prepare topping: Mix together the flour, sugar, baking powder, salt, butter and egg. Spoon this mixture over the fruit mixture. Place in the oven and bake until topping is lightly golden brown, about 30 minutes.

Easy Peach Pudding

3 canned or cooked peach halves
1/2 cup milk
2 tablespoons cornstarch

In a blender or food processor, put all of the ingredients and mix until smooth. In a saucepan over low heat cook mixture until thickened. Makes 1-1/2 cups. You can use coconut, nuts, granola or even peach chunks to decorate.

Peach Cooler

1 cup milk
1 cup peaches
dash of salt
2-3 drops almond extract, optional
1 cup vanilla ice cream

In a blender, combine all of the listed ingredients except the ice cream. Cover and process until smooth. Add the ice cream and blend just until mixed. Makes 2 servings

Peach Freezer Jam

2 cups pared crushed fresh peaches, about 2 pounds
3-1/4 cups sugar
1-3 ounce pouch liquid fruit pectin, about 7 tablespoons
3 tablespoons lemon juice

In a large bowl, combine peaches and sugar and mix well. Let stand 10 minutes. In a small bowl, combine the pectin and lemon juice. Pour this mixture over the peaches. Stir this mixture for about 3 minutes. Spoon this mixture into glass or plastic containers, cover and let stand at room temperature for 24 hours. Store in the freezer.

Peaches and Corn Flakes

This is a good recipe for when your at the bottom of the cereal box and very easy.

1 can (29 ounces) peach halves, drained and reserve 1/4 cup syrup

1/4 cup packed brown sugar

1/2 teaspoon ground cinnamon

1/4 teaspoon ground nutmeg

1/4 cup butter or margarine melted

1/4 cup coarsely crushed corn flakes

1/4 cup finely chopped pecans

Preheat oven to 350°. Put the peach halves cut side up in a 1-1/2 quart shallow baking dish. In a small bowl mix the reserved peach syrup, sugar, spices and 2 tablespoons butter. Pour this mixture over the peaches. Bake for 10 minutes. Mix the remaining melted butter, corn flakes and pecans. Spoon this over the peaches. Increase the oven temp to 400° and bake an additional 10 minutes.

Easy Peach Cake

3/4 cup cold butter or margarine
1 package yellow cake mix
2 egg yolks
2 cups (16 ounces) sour cream
1 can (29 ounces) sliced peaches, drained
1/2 teaspoon ground cinnamon
1 carton (8 ounces) frozen whipped topping, thawed

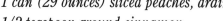

In a bowl, cut the butter into the cake mix until the mixture resembles coarse crumbs. Pat this mixture into a greased 13 x 9 x 2 inch baking pan. In another bowl, beat egg yolks; add the sour cream and mix well. Set aside 6-8 peach slices for garnish. Cut remaining peaches into 1 inch pieces. Stir the peaches into the sour cream mixture. Spread this over the crust, sprinkle with cinnamon. Bake at 350° for 25-30 minutes or until the edges begin to brown. Cool on a wire rack. Spread with whipped topping, garnish with reserved peaches. Store in the refrigerator. 12 servings.

Peach Chutney

1 large apple, chopped
1/3 cup seedless raisins
1 can (29 ounces) cling peach slices
1 cup chopped celery
1/4 cup chopped green pepper
1 tablespoon instant minced onion
3/4 cup cider vinegar
1/2 cup sugar
1/2 teaspoon salt
1/4 teaspoon ground ginger
Few grains of cayenne pepper

In a kettle combine all of the ingredients. Stir until blended. Cook uncovered, low heat about 1 hour or until syrup is thickened and chutney is desired consistency. Stir occasionally to prevent sticking. Ladle into clean hot jars cover tightly. When cool, store in the refrigerator. Makes 2 one pint jars.

Peach Butter

1 cup firm unsalted butter
1/2 cup confectioners sugar
1 package (10 ounces) frozen sliced peaches, thawed and cut into pieces

In a bowl add the butter, with an electric beater whip the butter gradually adding the confectioners sugar. To this add the peaches very slowly beating thoroughly. This is great on pancakes, french toast, waffles, muffins and bagels.

Peach Sundae Sauce

1/2 cup sugar
1 tablespoon cornstarch
Dash of salt
1 can (29 ounces) peach slices, drained and coarsely crushed
* (Reserve 1/2 cup syrup)*
1/2 cup orange juice
1 tablespoon lemon juice
1 piece (1 inch) preserved ginger, finely chopped

In a saucepan over medium heat, combine the sugar, cornstarch and salt. Blend in the peach syrup and fruit juices. Bring to a boil. Stir and cook until slightly thickened and clear. Stir in the peaches and ginger. Simmer this mixture for about 5 minutes. Cool. Great over ice cream or pound cake.

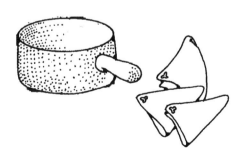

Peach-Maraschino Cherry Chutney

3/4 cup quartered maraschino cherries (about 30)
1 package (10 ounce) frozen peach slices, thawed, drained
  and cut into pieces
1/2 cup chopped walnuts
1 tablespoon finely chopped preserved ginger
2 tablespoons honey

In a small saucepan, mix all of the ingredients over low heat for about 8 minutes, stir occasionally. Cool. Serve as an accompaniment. Makes about 3 cups.

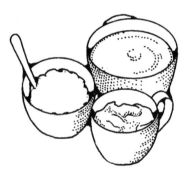

Peaches and Cherries for Meat

*1 can (16 ounces) water packed pitted tart cherries drained
(reserve the liquid)*
1 can (29 ounces) peach halves drained (reserve the syrup)
2 tablespoons red wine vinegar
1/3 cup honey
1 teaspoon ground cinnamon
4 whole cloves

In a saucepan, mix the cherry liquid, peach syrup, vinegar, honey, cinnamon and cloves. Bring this to a boil and then remove the pan from the heat. Add the cherries to the saucepan and let stand for several hours or overnight. Heat the marinade and bring to boiling, add the peach halves and heat thoroughly. Remove the peach halves with a slotted spoon and arrange cut side up. Fill each cavity with the cherries. Pour the juice over the peaches and cherries. Serve this with chicken or pork.

Barbecued Pork Chops and Peaches

6 pork chops, 1 inch thick
1 tablespoon vegetable shortening
1/4 cup lightly packed brown sugar
1 teaspoon ground cinnamon
1/2 teaspoon ground cloves
1 can (8 ounce) tomato sauce
6 canned cling peach halves drained
 (reserve 1/4 cup syrup)
1/4 cup cider vinegar
3/4 teaspoon salt
1/4 teaspoon pepper

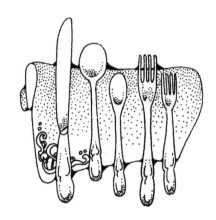

In a skillet brown the pork chops on both sides in hot shortening. In a bowl, blend the brown sugar, cinnamon and cloves with the tomato sauce, reserved peach syrup and vinegar. From the pan pour off the excess fat from the meat. Sprinkle the chops with the salt and pepper. Place a peach half on each pork chop and pour the sauce over all. Cover the skillet and simmer about 30 minutes or until the pork is tender. Baste occasionally with the sauce. Serves 6.

Peach and Strawberry Yogurt Drink

1 cup sliced strawberries
1 cup canned unsweetened, sliced peaches
1 cup plain yogurt
1-1/2 tablespoons sugar

In a food processor or blender add all of the ingredients, cover and blend until smooth. Pour into glasses and serve.

Coconut Peach Pie

1 9-inch pie shell
4-1/2 cups sliced fresh peaches
1/2 cup sugar
3 tablespoons flour
1/4 teaspoon nutmeg
1/8 teaspoon salt
1/4 cup orange juice
2 tablespoons butter
2 cups flaked coconut
1/2 cup evaporated milk
1 egg, beaten
1/4 teaspoon almond extract

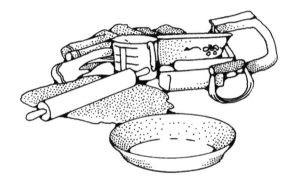

Preheat oven to 450°. In a bowl, mix together the peaches, sugar, flour, nutmeg, salt and orange juice. Place the peach mixture into the pie shell, dot with butter and bake for 15 minutes. In a bowl combine coconut, milk, egg and extract. Pour this over the hot peach mixture and reduce the oven temperature to 350°. Bake for 30 minutes or until the coconut is toasted. Chill the pie.

Quick Dessert Fruit Pie

1 prepared graham cracker crust
1 small container whipped topping
1/4 cup melted chocolate (optional)
2 cups fresh fruit, sliced peaches and/or plums

In the graham cracker crust, place the whipped topping. On the whipped topping place fruit and then drizzle the melted chocolate over the fruit. Serve and chill any leftovers.

PEARS

"There are many ways to enlarge your child's world. Love of books is best of all." Jacqueline Kennedy Onassis

Pear Coleslaw

2 cups chopped pears fresh or canned
4 teaspoons apple or pear juice
2 cups shredded green cabbage
1 cup shredded carrots
1 cup shredded red cabbage
1 green onion chopped
3 tablespoons mayonnaise
Salt and pepper to taste

In a medium bowl place the pears, cabbage, carrots and onions. Toss well. In a separate bowl combine the mayonnaise, liquid, salt and pepper. Whisk until smooth. Pour this dressing into the cabbage and toss, mixing well. Refrigerate and served chilled. Serves about 6.

Raspberry Pear Cobbler

1 package (10 ounces) frozen red raspberries, thawed
1/3 cup sugar
2 teaspoons cornstarch
1/4 teaspoon ground cinnamon
3 medium pears, peeled, cored and sliced
1 cup all purpose flour
1/2 cup sugar
1 teaspoon baking powder
1/4 teaspoon salt
1 egg, beaten
3/4 cup sour cream
2 tablespoons melted butter or margarine

Drain the raspberries and reserve the syrup. One cup syrup is needed, you may need to add water to make a cup. In a saucepan, combine 1/3 cup sugar, cornstarch and spice. Then add the raspberry syrup. Cook over medium heat stirring frequently until the mixture is thickened and bubbly. Stir in the berries and pears and heat them through. In a 1-1/2 quart baking dish pour the fruit mixture. In a bowl, combine the flour, 1/2 cup sugar, baking powder and 1/4 teaspoon salt. In a separate bowl, mix the egg, sour cream and butter. Add this to the flour mixture. Blend well. Drop this mixture by the spoonfuls on top of the hot fruit mixture. Bake at 350° for 30 minutes, until browned. Serves 6.

Pear Pineapple Butter

8 medium pears
1/2 cup water
2-1/2 cups sugar
1 can (8-1/4 ounces) crushed pineapple, undrained
1/2 cup honey
1/4 cup lemon juice

Core and slice the pears into a large pot with water. Cook uncovered until the pears are soft, about 20 minutes. Remove from the heat and puree the pears to measure 3-1/2 cups. Return to the pot and add the remaining ingredients and mix well. Boil gently uncovered for about 25 minutes stirring often. Remove from the heat. Pour into hot sterile jars, seal. Hot water bath for 10 minutes. Makes 5 half pints.

Pear Cranberry Crisp

1 cup rolled oats
1/2 cup packed brown sugar
3 tablespoons all purpose flour
1/2 teaspoon cinnamon
1/4 teaspoon salt
3 tablespoons butter or margarine, softened
5 ripe pears, peeled and cored
1 cup cleaned cranberries
3 tablespoons sugar
1 tablespoon fresh lemon juice

Preheat oven to 375°. In a bowl stir together the oats, brown sugar, flour, cinnamon and salt. Add the butter and blend together until crumbly. Slice the pears thin. In a 9 inch baking dish add the pears, cranberries, sugar and lemon juice. Toss gently. Sprinkle the oat mixture on top of the fruit. Bake for 1 hour or until the top is golden brown and the juices are bubbling around the edges. Cool and serve.

Pear Relish

12 large pears
7-8 bell peppers
8 medium white onions
1 quart vinegar
4 cups sugar
1 tablespoon turmeric
1 tablespoon salt
1 teaspoon black pepper

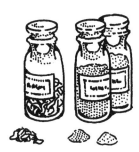

With a grinder, grind the pears, peppers and onions. Place this in a heavy kettle over medium heat. Add the remaining ingredients. Stir and bring this mixture to a boil for 2 minutes. Place in hot sterile jars and seal in a hot water bath or 10 minutes. Makes 5 quarts. This is great with pork.

Pear Apple Nut Conserve

1 quart pears, cored, peeled and diced
1 quart apples, cored, peeled and diced
2 lemons juiced and the rind grated
2 cups golden raisins
7 cups sugar
1 cup slivered walnuts

In a heavy kettle combine all of the ingredients except the nuts over medium heat. Cook, occasionally stirring for about 30 minutes. The mixture will be thick and clear. Add the nuts in the last 5 minutes of cooking. Pack in hot sterile pint jars and seal. Makes 4 pints.

Pear Chutney

4 cups fresh cranberries
1 cup raisins
1 medium white onion, finely chopped
3/4 cup brown sugar packed
1/3 cup cider vinegar
3 large garlic cloves, minced
2 teaspoons mustard seed
1/4 teaspoon ground ginger
1/4 teaspoon allspice
1/4 teaspoon ground cloves
1/4 teaspoon crushed red pepper flakes (for taste)
1 large pear peeled, cored and chopped

In a saucepan over medium, heat all of the ingredients except the pear. Bring this to a boil and reduce the heat to low. Cook uncovered stirring occasionally for 30 minutes. Then add the pear and cook an additional 10-15 minutes. Store in the refrigerator. Serve warm or cold with white meat.

Crumb Pear Pie

1 9-inch unbaked pie shell
2-1/2 pounds pears, peeled, cored and sliced
1 tablespoon lemon juice
2/3 cup sugar
1 teaspoon cinnamon
1/4 teaspoon mace
1-2 tablespoons flour

Topping:
1 cup flour
1/3 cup brown sugar
1/3 cup butter or margarine, softened

Preheat oven to 375°. In a bowl place the pears and lemon juice. Toss gently. In another bowl combine the sugar, cinnamon, mace and flour. Add this mixture to the pears and toss gently to mix. Place this mixture into the prepared pie shell. Combine the topping ingredients and sprinkle this over the top of the pears. Bake for 40-45 minutes or until the juice bubbles and top is browned, cool.

Pear Sauce

4 pears peeled, cored and quartered
1/2 cup sugar
1/2 cup water
Dash of ginger
2 teaspoons lemon juice
1/2 teaspoon grated lemon peel
1/4 teaspoon vanilla

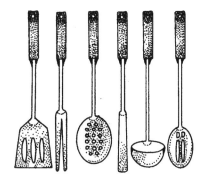

In a saucepan cook the pears with sugar and the water, covered until tender, about 30 minutes. Mash the pears and add the remaining ingredients. This is good with gingerbread and ice cream. Also dip for gingersnap cookies or graham crackers for kids.

Baked Pears

6 pears unpeeled, cored and halved
1/2 cup dark brown sugar
1/2 cup maple syrup
1/2 cup water
1/4 teaspoon ginger

Preheat oven to 325°. In a baking dish place your pears flat side down. In a bowl combine the rest of the ingredients and mix well. Take this mixture and pour it over the pears. Bake for 1 hour. You may have to add more water during the baking to prevent burning so watch the pears carefully.

Chocolate Ice Cream and Pears

6 ounces chocolate chips
1/2 cup light corn syrup
1/4 cup evaporated milk
1 tablespoon butter
1/4 teaspoon vanilla
1 quart vanilla ice cream
4 pears, peeled, cored, halved and cooked

In the top of a double boiler over medium heat melt the chocolate chips. Then stir in the corn syrup and mix well. Cool this mixture, then add the milk, butter and vanilla and mix well. In a saucepan with 1 tablespoon of water, cook pears until tender, remove from heat and cool. In 8 dessert dishes spoon in the ice cream. Then place a pear half in each dish. Spoon the chocolate sauce over the top and serve.

Pear Pineapple Pie

Pastry for a two crust pie
2 tablespoons flour
1/3 cup sugar
1/2 teaspoon salt
1/2 teaspoon ground nutmeg
5 cups thinly sliced pears
1/3 cup crushed pineapple well drained
2 tablespoons raisins
2 tablespoons lemon juice

Preheat oven to 375°. In a bowl, combine flour, sugar, salt and nutmeg. Toss the pears and remaining ingredients in a separate bowl. Gently place in the pie shell. Sprinkle flour mixture on top of pears. Roll out the top crust and place on the filling. Seal and crimp the edges. Bake for 50-60 minutes.

Pear Ginger Pie

Unbaked 9-inch pie shell
3/4 cup sugar
2 tablespoons flour
3/4 teaspoon ground ginger
1/4 teaspoon salt
3 ripe pears
2 tablespoons soft butter
2 eggs, separated
1 teaspoon grated lemon peel
3 tablespoons lemon juice
3/4 cup milk

Preheat oven to 425°. In a bowl, combine 1/4 cup sugar, 1 tablespoon flour, ginger and salt. Sprinkle this into the bottom of the pie shell. Peel and core your pears, slice thinly and lay slices over sugar-flour mixture. In a bowl, cream the butter with a mixer. Then add 1/2 cup sugar, 1 tablespoon flour. Add the egg yolks, lemon peel and juice. Beat thoroughly. Add milk and mix. Beat egg whites in a separate bowl until stiff. Fold this into the lemon mixture. Pour over the pears. Bake in a hot oven for 10 minutes; reduce heat to 350° and bake an additional 30 minutes.

Spice Pear Muffins

2 cups all purpose flour
1/2 cup packed brown sugar
2 teaspoons ground ginger
1 teaspoon baking soda
1 teaspoon ground cinnamon
1/2 teaspoon salt
1/8 teaspoon ground nutmeg
1/8 teaspoon ground cloves
1 egg
1 cup (8 ounce) plain yogurt
1/2 cup vegetable oil
3 tablespoons molasses
1-1/2 cups finely chopped peeled pears
1/2 cup raisins
1/2 cup chopped nuts

Preheat oven to 400°. In a large bowl combine all of the dry ingredients. In a different bowl, combine and beat the egg, yogurt, oil and molasses until smooth. Stir this mixture into the dry mixture and stir until just moistened. Then gently fold in the pears, raisins and nuts. Fill greased or paper lined muffin tins 2/3s full. Bake 10 to 20 minutes or until done depending on the size of the muffin tin. Cool on a wire rack.

Cheddar Cheese Pear Pie

4 large ripe pears, peeled, pared and sliced thin
1/3 cup sugar
1 tablespoon cornstarch
1/8 teaspoon salt
1 9-inch unbaked prepared pie crust

Topping:
1/2 - 3/4 cup shredded cheddar cheese
1/2 cup all purpose flour
1/4 cup melted butter or margarine
1/4 cup sugar
1/4 teaspoon salt

Preheat oven to 425°. In a bowl combine the first four ingredients and pour into the unbaked pie shell. In a small bowl combine all of the topping ingredients and mix until crumbly. Sprinkle this mixture over the pear filling. Bake for 25-35 minutes or until the crust is golden brown and the cheese is melted. Cool the pie on a wire rack.

Pear Marmalade

3 oranges, cut in quarters and de-seeded
6 ripe pears, peeled, cored and cut into pieces
1 large can of crushed pineapple
1 jar maraschino cherries
Sugar

Take the oranges with the peel on and pears through a food grinder. Measure the fruit and add one cup of sugar to each cup of fruit and mix. Add this mixture to a heavy pot. Add pineapple and mix. Cover over medium low heat until thick, stirring occasionally. Add the maraschino cherries at the last 5 minutes of cooking time. Seal in hot sterilized jars.

Pear Conserve

1 cup pears, peeled, cored and ground
1 cup apples, peeled, cored and ground
2 cups sugar
2 teaspoons pineapple extract

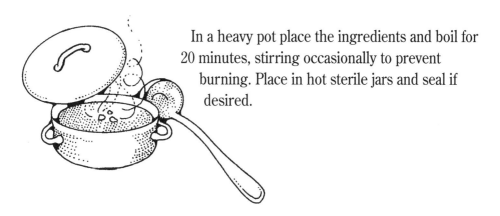

In a heavy pot place the ingredients and boil for 20 minutes, stirring occasionally to prevent burning. Place in hot sterile jars and seal if desired.

Sugar Pear Cake

This is from my friend Patti Neumann

1/2 cup butter
1 cup sugar
2 egg yolks
1-2/3 cups flour
1 teaspoon soda
1/2 teaspoon salt
1/4 cup buttermilk
1 cup mashed pears
1 teaspoon vanilla
1/2 cups chopped walnuts
2 egg whites
Powdered sugar

Preheat oven to 350°. Grease a 9 x 9 x 2 inch pan. In a medium bowl cream together the first three ingredients. Sift together the flour, soda and salt and add this to the butter mixture. Mix well. Add the milk slowly and the rest of the ingredients except the powder sugar. Bake for 30-40 minutes or until cake test done. Remove from oven and sprinkle with powdered sugar before serving.

Pear Chip Marmalade
This is from my friend Patti Neumann

2 pounds pears, peeled, cored and chopped
3 cups sugar
1 teaspoon whole cloves
1/3 cup shredded or candied ginger
2 medium lemons seeded and sliced thin
1/4 inch thick orange peel sliced finely and chopped

Place all of the ingredients together in a pot and let stand overnight or for several hours. Bring this mixture to a slow boil over medium heat, stirring. Then simmer for 1 hour. It will thicken upon standing and cooling.

Chocolate Pear Dip

1 milk chocolate bar broken into small pieces
2 tablespoons milk
1 medium pear cored and sliced

Place the chocolate pieces and milk into a small microwave safe bowl.
Microwave at medium for 30 seconds. Stir and microwave another 30 seconds.
Be careful not to burn. All microwaves differ in temp. Serve pear wedges with
the chocolate dipping sauce. This makes 4 servings unless you're a chocoholic.

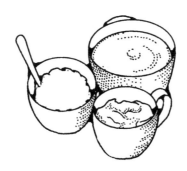

Pear Maple Glazed Pork Roast

3 fresh pears, halved and cored
3/4 cup maple flavored syrup
1/2 cup brown sugar
2 tablespoons prepared mustard
2 tablespoons butter
1 tablespoon whole cloves
2-1/2 to 3 pound rolled trimmed pork loin roast
Salt and pepper

Preheat oven to 325°. Place the pork roast in a shallow roasting pan. Season with salt and pepper. Roast the meat until the meat thermometer registers 170 degrees. It will take about 35 to 40 minutes per pound. While the meat is cooking; combine the maple syrup, brown sugar, mustard, butter and cloves in a pan over low heat until the sugar is dissolved. During the last 30 minutes of cooking the pork roast place the pears cut side up in the roasting pan with the pork. Baste the pears and pork frequently with the maple glaze. Serve the glazed pear halves as an accompaniment to the pork. This is great with brown rice or risotto. Serves about 6 people.

Pear Topped French Toast

3 tablespoons butter or margarine
2 tablespoons packed brown sugar
1/2 cup pineapple juice
1/8 teaspoon ground ginger
2 pears cored and thinly sliced
French Toast
Coconut

Melt butter in a skillet and add sugar until melted, stirring constantly. Stir in the pineapple juice and ginger and boil until the mixture is syrupy. Add the pears and turn to coat them and boil until the mixture is a little thicker. Cook over low heat for 5 to 10 minutes or until the pears are tender. Serve over French Toast and garnish with coconut if desired.

Easy Chocolate Pear Cake

1 package chocolate cake mix
2 medium pears cored and sliced
1/2 cup flour
1/4 cup packed brown sugar
1 teaspoon ground cinnamon
1/4 cup margarine

Preheat oven to 350°. Prepare the cake mix according to the package directions. Pour the batter into a greased 13 x 9 x 2 inch baking pan. Press sliced pears into the batter. In a small bowl, combine flour, brown sugar and cinnamon and cut in the butter. Sprinkle the mixture over the pears. Bake for 30 to 40 minutes until cake test done.

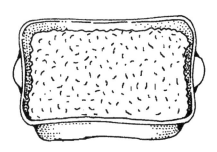

Raw Pear Cake

1 cup shortening
2 cups sugar
2-1/2 cups flour
1/2 teaspoon salt
1 teaspoon soda
1/2 cup water
4 eggs
1 teaspoon cinnamon
1 teaspoon allspice
1 teaspoon cloves
1 teaspoon vanilla
1 cup pecans chopped
2 cups pears chopped

Preheat oven to 375°. In a large bowl cream together the shortening and sugar, add the rest of the ingredients and mix well. In a greased and floured bunt pan, add the mixture and bake for about 1 hour until done.

Chocolate Pear Cake

3/4 cup butter or margarine
3/4 cup sugar
3 eggs
1/4 cup cocoa
1 tablespoon vanilla extract
1 cup all purpose flour
1/4 teaspoon salt
2 pears peeled, cored and sliced thin
Powder sugar
4 pear slices for garnish

Preheat oven to 375°. Grease an 11 inch baking pan or a tart pan. In a bowl cream butter with sugar until well blended. Add the eggs and beat until light and fluffy. Stir in the cocoa, vanilla, flour and salt. Mix well. Spread this mixture into your baking pan. Batter should be only 1/2 inch deep. Arrange your pear slices over the batter pressing the slices into the batter. Bake for 30-35 minutes. Cool and dust with powder sugar. Garnish with fresh pear slices.

Pear Pecan Bread

2 cups sugar
3/4 cup corn oil
3 eggs
3 cups flour
1/2 teaspoon baking powder
1 teaspoon baking soda
1/2 teaspoon salt
1 teaspoon cinnamon
1/2 teaspoon nutmeg
2 cups fresh grated pears
1 cup chopped pecans
1/2 teaspoon vanilla

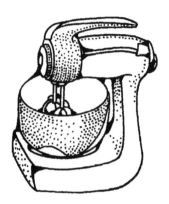

Preheat oven to 325°. In a bowl, cream the sugar and oil, then beat in the eggs. Sift together flour, baking powder, soda, salt and spices and add to the egg mixture. With a mixer, beat on medium speed until well mixed. Add the pears, mixing well. Stir in the pecans and vanilla. Bake in 2 greased, floured loaf pans for 1 hour or until cake test done.

Pear Muffins

4 large pears, peeled, cored and diced
1 cup sugar
1/2 cup vegetable oil
2 large eggs beaten
2 teaspoons vanilla
2 cups flour
2 teaspoons baking soda
2 teaspoons cinnamon
1 teaspoon nutmeg
1 teaspoon salt
1 cup raisins
1 cup chopped walnuts

Preheat oven to 325°. Prepare muffin tin by using muffin cups or greasing the tin. In a medium bowl mix the pears and sugar. Blend oil, eggs and vanilla in a large bowl. Combine flour, baking soda, cinnamon, nutmeg and salt in a separate bowl. Stir the pear mixture into the egg mixture, then mix in the dry ingredients. Fold in the raisins and walnuts. Do not over mix. Spoon batter into muffin tin, makes about 16-18 muffins. Bake for 30 minutes.

Pear Citrus Fruit Jam

2-1/2 pounds pears
1 orange
1 lemon
3/4 cup drained crushed pineapple
5-1/2 cups sugar

Peel and core pears. Grind the pears, orange and lemon including the rinds, using the coarse blade of a chopper. In a bowl add the fruits, pineapple and sugar, stir well. In a heavy pot place this mixture and cook over medium heat until boiling. Cook for about 20 minutes, stirring occasionally over low heat. Pour into hot sterilized jars and seal. Makes about 9 six-ounce jars.

Spiced Pears with Lime

1 can (29 ounces) Bartlett pear halves, drained
1 cup reserved pear juice
1 cup light corn syrup
2 pieces (3 inch each) stick cinnamon
2 teaspoons whole cloves
1/2 cup lime juice

Combine the reserved pear syrup with corn syrup and the spices in a saucepan. Bring to a boil, stirring occasionally to mix well. Boil about 10 minutes. Stir in the lime juice and add the pear halves, bring the syrup to simmering. Remove from heat, set aside to allow the pears to absorb the flavor.

Pears and Pork Chops

6 pork chops cut 3/4 to 1 inch thick
1/2 teaspoon salt
1/8 teaspoon pepper
6 thin lemon slices
12 thin onion slices
3 pears, halved and cored
3/4 cup lightly packed brown sugar
1/2 cup lemon juice
1/2 cup warm water
1/3 cup soy sauce
1/2 teaspoon ground ginger

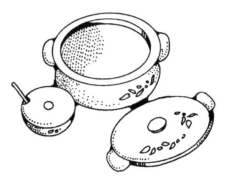

In a skillet, brown the pork chops on both sides. Drain off any fat. Season the pork chops with the salt and pepper. Put a lemon slice and two onion slices on each chop. Place the pear halves cut-side down in skillet around the chops. Combine brown sugar with the lemon juice, water, soy sauce and ginger and pour over all. Cover, basting frequently with the sauce and cook over low heat about 20 minutes, then turn pears cut side up and cook 20 minutes longer or until pork is tender. 6 Servings.

Cranberry-Pear Cake

1/2 cup butter
4 large eggs
2-1/2 cups all purpose flour, sifted
1 tablespoon baking powder
1 teaspoon soda
1/4 teaspoon salt
1-1/4 cups granulated sugar

1-1/2 teaspoons vanilla extract
1/4 cup buttermilk
3 cups pears, peeled and coarsely
   chopped
1 cup cranberries, coarsely chopped
Confectioner's sugar for dusting

Let the butter and eggs stand at room temperature for 30 minutes. In a small mixing bowl, combine baking powder, soda and salt, set aside. In a large mixing bowl, beat the butter with and electric mixer on medium speed for half a minute. Gradually add granulated sugar to butter about 2 tablespoons at a time, beating on medium to high speed for a total of 5 minutes. Add vanilla and blend again. Add the eggs, one at a time, beating for 1 minute after each egg. Beat in the buttermilk. Gradually add the flour mixture to creamed butter mixture beating low to medium until combined. Fold in the pears and cranberries. Spoon batter into a greased floured 10 inch fluted tube pan or a spring form pan. Bake at 350° for 50-55 minutes. Cool for 15 minutes and then remove from the pan. Dust with powdered sugar before serving.

Nut Baked Pears

6 medium pears, peeled, halved and cored
1-1/2 cups water
1/3 cup white grape juice
1/2 cup finely chopped almond, walnuts or pecans
2 tablespoons brown sugar
1/8 teaspoon almond extract

Preheat oven to 350°. In a 13 x 9 x 2 inch baking pan combine the water and juice. Place the pears flat side down in the pan and then pour the liquid over the pears. Cover and bake for 35-45 minutes. Remove from the oven and uncover. Carefully turn the pears over in the baking dish so the flat side is up. In a bowl, combine the nuts of your choice, brown sugar and extract, mix well. Spoon this mixture into the cavities of the pears. Bake uncovered for an additional 5-7 minutes. Serve warm. This is good with ham or a pork dinner as an accompaniment.

Pear Zucchini Bread

2 cups chopped peeled pears
1 cup shredded zucchini
1 cup sugar
1 cup packed brown sugar
3 eggs beaten
1 cup vegetable oil
1 tablespoon vanilla extract
2 cups all purpose flour
1 cup whole wheat flour
2 teaspoons pumpkin pie spice
1 teaspoon baking soda
1/2 teaspoon baking powder
1/2 teaspoon salt
1/2 cup chopped pecans

Preheat oven to 350°. Grease two loaf pans. In a large bowl, combine the first seven ingredients. Combine in another bowl the flours, pie spice, baking soda, baking powder and salt. Mix together. Turn this mixture into the pear mixture until well blended. Fold in the nuts. Pour into the loaf pans and bake for 55-60 minutes until toothpick is inserted and comes out clean. Remove from pans and cool on a wire rack.

PLUMS

"Children who grow up to adulthood and left others to a place of worth & value is the greatest harvest any parent can produce."
Reverend Tracy Lewis

Plum Pie

4 cups sliced fresh plums
1/2 cup sugar
1/4 cup all purpose flour
1/4 teaspoon salt
1/4 teaspoon ground cinnamon
1 tablespoon lemon juice
1 9-inch unbaked deep dish pie pastry shell

Topping:
1/2 cup sugar
1/2 cup all purpose flour
1/4 teaspoon ground cinnamon
1/4 teaspoon ground nutmeg
3 tablespoons cold butter or margarine

In a bowl, combine all six ingredients and toss to mix well. Pour all of these ingredients into the pastry shell. For the topping, combine the sugar, flour, cinnamon and nutmeg. Cut in the butter until the mixture resembles coarse crumbs. Sprinkle this over the pie filling. Bake at 375° for 50-60 minutes, or until bubbly and golden brown. To prevent the edges of the crust from burning cover the edges of the crust with some foil for the last 20 minutes of baking time.

Simple Rice-Plum Pudding

2 cans of rice pudding
1 cup prepared whipped topping
Canned purple plums

In a bowl, mix the rice pudding and whipped topping. Spoon this mixture into individual service dishes. Spoon the plums over the pudding. If desired, garnish each serving with additional whipped topping and sprinkle of ground cinnamon and drizzle the plum juice.

Red Plum Ketchup

8 ounces or 1 cup of red pitted plums
1 shallot, chopped
1/3 cup chopped dried dates
1 tablespoon vinegar
1 teaspoon cornstarch
2 tablespoons water

In a pan boil the plums, shallot, dates and vinegar until soft. Process in a blender, making a puree, then return it back to the pan. In a separate bowl, mix cornstarch and water until dissolved and add to the puree. Boil for 10 minutes, stirring. Pour into sterilized jars, top with lids and process in a hot water bath for 25 minutes. Let cool and store in a cool place. This ketchup is a great dip for any type of meat.

Poached Plums

1 pound fresh plums
1/2 cup sugar
1-1/2 cups water
2 thin slices of lemon

Take the plums and cut them in half. Remove the pits. In a saucepan over medium heat, combine sugar and the water. Bring this to a boil and continue boiling for 5-6 minutes. Add the plums and lemon to the sugar mixture. Return to a boil and reduce the heat. Simmer for 3 to 4 minutes. Remove from the heat, cool and refrigerate.

Plum Conserve

5 pounds blue plums
2 oranges
1 lemon
1 pound chopped raisins
1/2 pound chopped walnut meats
3 pounds of sugar

In a heavy pot add the washed, peeled and pitted plums. Chop the oranges with the peel. Grate the rind and juice the lemon. Add the raisins and walnuts. Mix thoroughly and boil until quite thick, about 40 minutes. Seal in hot sterile jars.

Grilled Pork and Plums

1 tablespoon fresh chopped sage or 1 teaspoon dry sage
1/2 teaspoon salt
1/2 teaspoon sugar
1/4 teaspoon paprika
6 pork chops, 1/2 inch thick with fat trimmed off
6 plums
1/4 cup honey
2 tablespoons lime juice
1 teaspoon Dijon style mustard

In a bowl mix the sage, salt, sugar and paprika for a dry rub. Take your chops and put them in a shallow dish and rub the mixture into the meat on both sides. Cover and refrigerate at least 1 hour or overnight. Heat your grill to medium hot. Place the grill rack about 4 inches above the coals. Cut each plum in half and remove the pits. In a small bowl combine the honey, lime juice and mustard. Place the chops on the grill for about 4-5 minutes on each side or until done. Place the plums on the grill also and cook, turning until lightly brown and soft. Brush the chops and plums with the honey mixture and grill until glazed looking. When done transfer to a serving platter. Drizzle the remaining honey if any left and serve.

Plum Sauce for Meats

1 pound red or purple plums, pitted and chopped
1/2 cup firmly packed light brown sugar
1/3 cup water
1 tablespoon soy sauce
1 teaspoon finely grated peeled fresh ginger root
1/4 teaspoon salt
1/3 cup ketchup
1 teaspoon lemon juice

In a heavy sauce pan, cook over medium heat the plums, brown sugar, water, soy sauce, ginger root and salt to boiling, stirring occasionally. Reduce heat to low and simmer plum mixture until very soft, about 10-15 minutes. Remove the plum mixture from the heat. Stir in the ketchup and lemon juice. In a food processor, process this mixture until smooth. Stop occasionally to scrape the container. Pour the plum sauce into a small bowl and serve warm or cold. Cover and refrigerate.

Plum Cream Pie

1 (8 ounce) package cream cheese, softened
1/4 cup light corn syrup
1 cup cold milk
1 package (3-3/4 ounce) of vanilla pudding mix
1 9-inch prepared graham cracker crust
1 cup pitted sliced plums
1/4 cup red currant jelly, melted

In a bowl, place the cream cheese and beat at high speed until the cheese is smooth. Gradually beat in the corn syrup until light and fluffy, set aside. In a separate bowl, mix the milk and pudding for two minutes. Fold this mixture into the cheese mixture and then place this mixture into the graham crust. Refrigerate for 2 hours or until set. Arrange the plums on the top of the pie and brush the fruit with jelly. Serve.

Plum Kuchen

1-1/2 cups flour
4 tablespoons sugar
2 teaspoons baking powder
1/2 teaspoon salt
3 tablespoons butter
1 egg
6 tablespoons milk
5 plums pitted and halved

Topping:
1/2 cup brown sugar
1 teaspoon cinnamon
1/4 cup flour
1/4 cup soft butter

Preheat oven to 450°. In a bowl cut the butter into the flour, sugar, baking powder and salt until crumbly. In a small bowl beat the egg and milk together. Slowly pour this into the crumb mixture and stir. In an 8 inch buttered square baking dish spread this mixture. Then place the plums cut side up in the baking dish. In a bowl combine the topping ingredients and sprinkle this over the top of the plums. Bake for 25 to 30 minutes.

Plum Muffins

3/4 of a pound of plums, peeled, pitted and chopped
2-1/2 cups flour
2 teaspoons baking soda
1/2 teaspoon salt
1 cup sugar
1/4 cup melted butter or margarine
2 eggs slightly beaten
1/2 cup milk
1/2 cup chopped walnuts
1 tablespoon sugar

Preheat oven to 400°. In a bowl, gently toss the plums with 1 tablespoon flour. In a large bowl, combine the flour, baking soda, salt and 1 cup sugar. In a separate bowl, stir the butter, eggs and milk until smooth. Combine the dry ingredients slowly to the liquid. Stir until just moistened. To this mixture fold in the plums and walnuts. Spoon the batter into muffin cups 2/3 full. Sprinkle 1 tablespoon of the sugar over the top of the batter. Bake 20-25 minutes. Makes 18 muffins.

Plum Pasta Salad

8 ounces pasta bows cooked until done
4 nectarines sliced thin
3 small zucchini grated
2 cups crumbled feta cheese
1/2 cup seedless green grapes halved
3 plums pitted and sliced thin
Salt and pepper to taste
2/3 cup olive oil
1 tablespoon chopped chives, fresh
1/4 cup chopped fresh parsley
1/4 cup chopped fresh basil

In a bowl, toss together the pasta, fruits, zucchini and cheese. In a bowl, blend together the remaining ingredients until coated. Then add this to the pasta and toss until well mixed. Chill and serve.

Plum Pear Relish

32 medium plums (2 pounds)
3 medium pears (1 pound)
3 cups sugar

Pit the plums and core the pears. With a food grinder coarsely grind the fruit. Measure 5 cups of the fruit mixture. In a heavy kettle stir together the fruit and sugar. Bring this to a full boil. Boil hard for 10-15 minutes stirring frequently. This mixture will become thick. Remove from the heat and quickly skim off the foam with a metal spoon. Pour the relish into hot sterile jars and seal. Makes 5 half pints. This relish is a great accompaniment for pork, chicken or turkey.

Graham Plum Pie

1 prepared graham cracker crust
6-8 plums pitted and sliced thin
1/2 cup packed brown sugar
2 tablespoons all purpose flour
1/2 teaspoon ground cinnamon

Preheat oven to 375°. In the pie crust arrange the plums into the crust evenly. In a bowl, combine the sugar, flour and cinnamon. Sprinkle this over the plums and bake 20 minutes or until the fruit is tender.

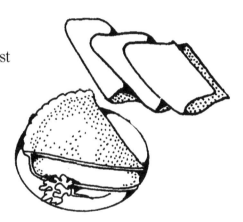

PRUNES

"The most precious fruit one's life can bear is not that of knowing you are loved but knowing you have loved others."
Reverend Tracy Lewis

Chicken Breast in Prune Sauce

2 tablespoons olive oil
4 boneless chicken breasts skinned
Salt and pepper
1/2 cup finely chopped onion
2 or 3 cloves minced garlic
1 cup chicken broth
1/2 cup chopped prunes
1/3 cup balsamic vinegar
1/2 teaspoon crushed dried thyme

In a large skillet, heat the oil over medium heat until hot. Season the chicken with salt and pepper to taste. Place the chicken in the skillet for about 10 minutes until brown and cooked. Transfer the chicken to a platter and keep warm. Add the onion and garlic to the pan and cook for 3 to 5 minutes until the onion is softened. Stir in the chicken broth, prunes, vinegar, thyme and salt and pepper. Bring this mixture to a boil and cook over high heat. Reduce heat to medium and cook until the sauce is reduced to 1/2. Spoon this mixture over the warm chicken and serve.

Lemon Prune Pie

1 9-inch baked pie pastry
3/4 cup granulated sugar
2 tablespoons cornstarch
Dash of salt
3/4 cup cold water
2 egg yolks, slightly beaten
1 teaspoon lemon peel, grated
3 tablespoons fresh lemon juice
1 cup soft prunes, chopped
1 tablespoon butter or margarine
1 cup sour cream

Combine the sugar, cornstarch and salt in a saucepan, then gradually add the water, stirring after each addition. Stir in the egg yolks, lemon peel, lemon juice and chopped prunes. Cook over medium heat until thickened and bubbly. Boil one minute and remove from the heat. Stir in the butter and let cool to room temperature, then blend in the sour cream and spoon the filling into the baked pie pastry. Refrigerate, cover until ready to serve.

Prune Cake

1/2 cup butter flavored shortening
1 cup sugar
2 eggs beaten
2 cups all purpose flour
1 teaspoon baking soda
1 teaspoon ground cinnamon
3/4 teaspoon salt
1/4 teaspoon ground allspice
1/4 teaspoon ground nutmeg
1 cup prune juice
1 cup finely chopped prunes
Confectioners sugar

Preheat oven to 350°. In a bowl, cream the shortening and sugar until fluffy. Add the eggs and continue beating until mixed well. In a separate bowl, combine all of the ingredients except confectioners sugar and mix well. Slowly add this mixture to the creamed mixture along with the prune juice until well mixed. Stir in the prunes. Pour the batter into a greased 8 x 9 inch cake pan or bunt pan. Bake for 40-45 minutes until the cake tests done. Cool and dust with confectioners sugar if desired.

Chocolate Covered Prunes

48 dried pitted prunes, about 1 pound
48 whole almond or walnut halves
2 cups (16 ounces) semisweet chocolate chips
2 tablespoons creamy peanut butter

Take each pitted prune and stuff with a nutmeat (almond or walnut). When completed, melt the chocolate chips in a microwave-safe bowl and mix well. Dip the prunes in the mixture and place on wax paper to harden. Store in the refrigerator.

Spiced Prunes

1 pound dried pitted prunes
2 cups water
1 teaspoon ground cinnamon
1 teaspoon ground cloves
1/2 teaspoon ground ginger
3 tablespoons lemon juice

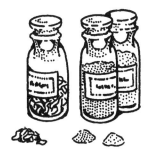

In a saucepan over medium heat, combine prunes, water, cinnamon, cloves and ginger. Stir and bring mixture to a boil. Remove pan from the heat, cover and let stand until cool. When cool stir in the lemon juice. Makes 8 servings.

Prune Waldorf Salad

3/4 cup mayonnaise
3 tablespoons orange juice
3 cups chopped red apple
8 ounces cubed turkey or chicken
1 cup chopped prunes
3/4 cup chopped celery
1/2 cup chopped walnuts
Lettuce leaves

In a medium bowl, combine the mayonnaise and juice, whisk. Then stir in the apples, meat, prunes, celery and walnuts. Coat this mixture well. Chill in the refrigerator. Serve on lettuce. Makes 6 servings.

Prune Peanut Butter Bars

1 cup packed brown sugar
1/2 cup crunchy peanut butter
2 tablespoons butter or margarine, softened
1/2 cup milk
1 egg
1 teaspoon vanilla extract
1 cup rolled oats
1-1/2 cups all purpose flour
1 teaspoon baking powder
1/2 teaspoon salt
1 cup chopped prunes
Powder sugar

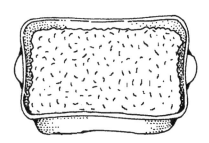

Preheat oven to 350°. Grease a 13 x 9 inch baking pan. In a bowl, beat together sugar, peanut butter and butter on medium speed until creamy. Add milk, egg and vanilla. Beat well. Combine the oats, flour, baking powder and salt. Add this to the sugar mixture, mixing on low speed until blended. Stir in the prunes. Press this mixture evenly into the pan and bake 25 minutes or until golden brown. Cool in pan and sprinkle with powder sugar. Cut into bars.

Peanut Butter Prune Muffins

3/4 cup sugar
1/2 cup creamy peanut butter
2 tablespoons vegetable oil
1 cups ripe bananas
1 egg, lightly beaten
1 tablespoon lemon juice
1-1/2 cups all purpose flour
2 teaspoons baking powder
1/2 teaspoon salt
1 cup chopped prunes
3 tablespoons chopped nuts

Preheat oven to 350°. Line 12 muffin cups with paper baking cups. In a medium bowl, beat together sugar, peanut butter and oil until creamy. Add the bananas, egg and lemon juice. Beat until blended. Combine flour, baking powder and salt. Add this to the sugar mixture until just moistened. Gently stir in the prunes. Fill the muffin cups 3/4 full and sprinkle the nut on top. Bake for 20 minutes or until cake test done.

Stuffed Ham with Fruit

1-5 pound smoked picnic ham
1 cups seedless raisins
2 cups pitted prunes
3 cups dried apricots
2 cups orange juice

Debone the ham or have your butcher do it. In a large mixing bowl, soak the fruit with the juice for 4 hours or longer, stir occasionally. Take this fruit mixture and fill the cavity of the boned ham. Bake at 350° for 2-1/2 hours.

Baked Chicken with Prunes

1 cup pitted prunes
1 cup water
3 pounds of chicken
1 tablespoon butter or margarine
Salt and pepper to taste

In a saucepan combine prunes and water, bring to a boil, then reduce the heat to low and simmer for 15 minutes or until the prunes are soft. In a food processor, puree the prunes and 2 tablespoons of the liquid from the prunes. Set aside. Preheat oven to 450°. Place chicken on a large heavy-duty aluminum foil sheet and rub the chicken with the butter, salt and pepper. Spread the prune puree over the chicken. Take the foil and bring it up closing the edges to seal well. Place this in a shallow baking dish and bake for 45 minutes. Carefully open the chicken and baste with the prune puree. Reduce the oven temperature to 400° and continue baking for 15 minutes, basting every 5 minutes. Serves 4. This is great served with sweet potatoes.

Prune Sticky Buns

1/2 cup packed brown sugar divided
1/4 cup plus 1 tablespoon light corn syrup, divided
2 tablespoons butter or margarine
1 loaf frozen bread defrosted
1/2 cup chopped prunes
1/2 teaspoon cinnamon

In a small saucepan, heat 1/4 cup sugar, 1/4 cup corn syrup and the butter over medium low heat until the sugar is dissolved, stirring frequently. Spoon this mixture into 12 well greased muffin cups. On a floured surface, roll out the bread dough to a 16 x 10 inch rectangle. Brush the remaining corn syrup over the dough. Combine the remaining sugar, prunes and cinnamon and sprinkle this evenly onto the dough leaving 1/2 inch around the dough clean. Beginning at the long end, roll the dough into a cylinder tube shape. Pinch the edges to seal. Cut into 12 pieces, place, cut side up, in muffin cups. Cover the dough with a towel or plastic to let rise until doubled, about 30 minutes. Preheat oven to 350°. Bake buns 15 to 20 minutes or until done. Invert the muffins onto serving platter.

MIXED FRUIT

"Get your family involved in cooking together and give them memories that they can pass on." Joan Bestwick

Hot Fruit Compote

1 can (20 ounces) pineapple chunks
2 cups fresh or canned peaches, peeled, pitted and sliced
2 cups fresh or canned pears, peeled, cored and sliced
1 jar maraschino cherries

Preheat oven to 350°. In a 13 x 9 x 2 inch baking pan arrange your fruit. Set aside.

Sauce:
1/3 cup sugar
2 tablespoons cornstarch
1/4 teaspoon salt
1/2 cup light corn syrup
1 cup orange juice

To make your sauce, combine all the ingredients in a saucepan over medium heat and boil. Remove from heat and pour the sauce over the fruit compote. Bake for 30 minutes or until the fruit is tender if fresh fruit is used.

Fruit Bake

1 large jar chunky applesauce
1 small can sliced peaches
1 small can sliced pears
1 small can pineapple chunks
1 cup white raisins
1/4 cup butter
1/4 to 1/2 cup brown sugar to taste
1 or 2 teaspoons cinnamon to taste

Preheat oven to 350°. Line a 9 x 13 inch pan with applesauce. Arrange the rest of the fruit on top. Dot the fruit with the butter. Combine the brown sugar and cinnamon and sprinkle over the top of the fruit. Bake for 45 to 60 minutes until bubbly.

Fruit Pancake

3 tablespoons butter or margarine, melted
1/2 cup flour
1/2 cup milk
4 eggs
1/8 teaspoon salt
1 or 2 fresh peaches or plums, peeled, sliced and pitted
Powder sugar
Maple syrup

Preheat oven to 425°. In a medium bowl, mix with a mixer or whisk the flour, milk, eggs and salt until smooth. Then add the melted butter and mix. Pour this mixture into a pie plate and bake for about 25 minutes or until the pancake is puffy and golden brown. Remove pancake from the oven, top with fresh fruit, sprinkle with powder sugar. Cut into wedges and serve. Top with maple syrup.

Summer Fruit Chutney

2 pounds ripe fresh nectarines, halved, pitted and diced
1 pound ripe fresh plums, halved, pitted and diced
1 pound ripe fresh peaches, halved, pitted and diced
3 cups diced onions
1-1/2 cups light corn syrup
1 cup firmly packed brown sugar
1 cup raisins
2 teaspoons lemon rind
3 tablespoons lemon juice
1 teaspoon salt
1 teaspoon ground ginger
1 teaspoon ground allspice

In a big heavy kettle, combine all of the ingredients. Stir frequently and bring the mixture to a boil over high heat. Boil gently uncovered, stirring frequently about 50 to 60 minutes or until thickened. Ladle into hot sterile jars, seal. Use a hot water bath for 5 minutes.

The Old Watermelon Boat

1 medium watermelon well chilled

To prepare the watermelon boat, cut a thin slice of rind off the bottom of the watermelon so that it will sit flat. Now slice off the top part of the melon. Now you can cut it straight across or you can get creative and fancy. Make a boat, basket, or whatever you choose. Carefully scoop out the watermelon and remove the seeds. Place watermelon shell back into the refrigerator and keep chilled.

In a bowl combine:
3 cups seedless grapes
3-4 peaches, pitted, peeled and sliced
4-5 plums, pitted and sliced
2 cups blueberries
4 kiwi fruit, peeled and sliced
2 cups strawberries, hulled and sliced
2 peeled and sliced bananas

Put the combined fruit in the watermelon and refrigerate any excess fruit and refill the melon as the fruit disappears. You can use any combinations of fruits as listed above. This should on an average serve 20 people.

Creamy Fruit Layered Salad

1-8 ounce carton of strawberry yogurt
4 ounces of cream cheese, softened
1 tablespoon sugar
2 teaspoons lemon juice
1/4 teaspoon almond extract
1/2 of an 8 ounce carton of whipped topping
8 cups of fruit cut-up into bite size pieces (peaches, pears,
   plums, grapes, apples)
3 tablespoons sliced toasted almonds

In a medium mixing bowl, gradually stir or whisk the yogurt in the cream cheese until it is smooth. Stir in the sugar, lemon juice and extract. Mix well. Fold in the dessert topping. In a large 2-1/2 quart clear serving bowl, layer half the fruit, then half of the yogurt mixture. Repeat and top with additional whipped topping if desired and the almonds. Chill until serving. Serves about 12 to 14.

Peach Plum Pie

2 cups sliced peaches, peeled and pitted
2 cups sliced plums, peeled and pitted
1 tablespoon lemon juice
1/4 teaspoon almond extract
1-1/2 cups sugar
1/4 cup quick cooking tapioca
1 teaspoon grated lemon peel
1/4 teaspoon salt
9-inch pastry for a double pie crust
2 tablespoons butter

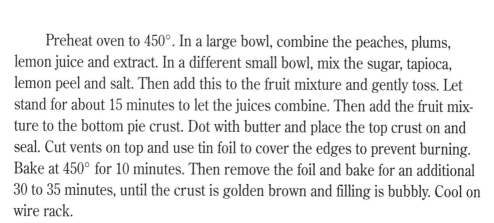

Preheat oven to 450°. In a large bowl, combine the peaches, plums, lemon juice and extract. In a different small bowl, mix the sugar, tapioca, lemon peel and salt. Then add this to the fruit mixture and gently toss. Let stand for about 15 minutes to let the juices combine. Then add the fruit mixture to the bottom pie crust. Dot with butter and place the top crust on and seal. Cut vents on top and use tin foil to cover the edges to prevent burning. Bake at 450° for 10 minutes. Then remove the foil and bake for an additional 30 to 35 minutes, until the crust is golden brown and filling is bubbly. Cool on wire rack.

INDEX

Love the Lord with ALL your heart & he will direct your path. Words to live by from Jenna Browning Townsend.

Life's Little Peaches, Pears, Plums & Prunes Cookbook

Favorite Recipes

Favorite Recipes

Notes

Notes

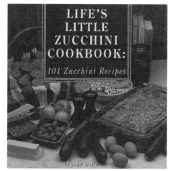

ISBN 0-932212-94-8

ISBN 1-892384-00-0

ISBN 1-892384-05-1

Look for Joan Bestwick's *Life's Little Zucchini Cookbook, Life's Little Rhubarb Cookbook* and *Life's Little Berry Cookbook* also by Avery Color Studios, Inc.

Avery Color Studios, Inc. has a full line of Great Lakes oriented books, puzzles, cookbooks, shipwreck and lighthouse maps, lighthouse posters and Fresnel lens model.

For a full color catalog call:
1-800-722-9925

Avery Color Studios, Inc. products are available at gift shops and bookstores throughout the Great Lakes region.